1

"Why Black why not white.

It does not matter if you are Black or White; you can still bless your World!

CONTENTS:

Why black why not white.

About The Author:

Shalom has brought, joy and peace into many lives in his generation. He is trained as a Real Estate Consultant. He studied SOP Theology with MFM, Business studies with Refus Giwe Polytechnic owo, Graphic design and multimedia with Edusa SA...And currently studying BA Multimedia in Digital Visual Art with university of South Africa UNISA. And a psychologist by career.

Also he is associate pastor at Enthoes family church situated at Rooihuiskraal Centurion. He is a partner with Kenneth

Copeland ministries. He is the CEO of Adebisi Shalom Trading Enterprises [Aste SA] and the director of Adebisi Shalom Leadership Institute [Asli SA] which is based in Rooihuiskraal Centurion South Africa.

His vision is to enable any men from any race to become who God has destined them to be.

Dedication: I dedicate this book, *Why Black Why Not White* to God Almighty. I gave Him the glory for making it possible for this dream to become a reality.

Proofread: By Pastor Chris Van Ransburg. The resident Pastor Entheos Family Church.

ISBN Number: 978-0-9947055-1-8

Introduction:

Why black why not white: Is based in inspirational, faith building and motivating any one that may desire to achieve his or her purpose in life.

It does not matter the background, race and what an individual has been through in life! And all the negative experiences that may have come across their path and journey from their childhood to their adulthood maybe? And with all things, they thought

may yield to substantial progress and result! Which has not yielded to the result of their expectations.

At some point? They thought they have been forgotten and neglected in their journey of achieving their purpose and knowing the existences of the reasons why they are living and exit in life.

Also. Due to their reasons of not been able in knowing or achieving the result of their purpose? They thought they are created blank and neglected by God! The creator of humans.

And that has been making them to choose all what they thought is right to do, in order for achieving success and living in the atmosphere of those that has been experiencing and achieving their purpose and living in

their perfect ordain will of
God, for their life.

Also. Two stories were share
from the scripture! The first
story is about a widow in the
book of 2 kings. The wife of
a prophet, which her husband
left debts for her, before
his death. And she finds it
so difficulty to pay her
debts.

Also, she received a
prophetic declaration from
the man of God to borrow
empty vessels! Which she did.
And she was instructed to
pour the jar of oil that was
left for her and her son,
into the empty vessels. And
there was a divine
multiplication, and she used
the proceed of the money of
the oil in paying her depth.

The second story can be found
in the Book of Genesis.
Chapter 32 vs 24-30. Regard

to Jacob having a divine
intervention with the angel
of God, and that leads to
the changing of his name and
being impacted to approach
his future with divine
intervention.

Also the children of Zebedee
how they approach Jesus and
imitating him.

Why Black Why Not White

In blessing your world, your
background does not matter. Where
you came from also does not matter.
Neither does your skin colour and hair

type have anything to do with the vision God has given you.

Blessing your world has to do with what the Bible says in Jeremiah1:5. 'Before *I formed thee in the belly, I knew thee; and before thou camest forth out of the womb I sanctified thee, and I ordained thee a prophet unto the nations*' Are you Black or White? We all know that some of the place of birth of a black man has to do with a background of bad reputation and a place of the less cultivated class, and lower moral type.

Sometime ago, I was preaching about 'Hometown' , and I took the text from the book of John Chapter 1 vs. 43-45, it says, '...the **next day He decided to leave for Galilee, Jesus found Philip and told him follow me. Now Philip was** *from Bethsaida, the hometown of Andrew and Peter. Philip found Nathanael and told him, we have found the One Moses wrote about in the Law [and so did the prophet]: Jesus the son of Joseph, from Nazareth. Can anything good come out of Nazareth? Nathanael asked him, Come and see, Philip answered.*

Beloved what is a Hometown? A Hometown is known as:

- a place of your destiny
- a place of your birth
- a place of your upbringing

According to the dictionary point of view? A Hometown is:

- The town or city in which a person live or was born, or from which a person comes from
- The town or city of one′s birth, race, rearing or main residence

No matter the race you may have come out from, either Black or White, it does not have to do with the divine assignment which God has given you to accomplish on earth. Remember every race has its own background. The Theologians have shared more light on Nazareth, a place I call home town.

It is a wonder that Nazareth, a village that it was, was chosen by God as the hometown of His beloved son, Jesus. It was the place of birth of Joseph and

Mary, the parents of our Lord Jesus Christ, also a place where our Lord Jesus Christ grew up from.

This explains the fact that Divinity is always found where it is least expected. 1 Cor 1 vs. 27, Choosing Nazareth as the hometown of His son is also a reflection of Jesus' humble upbringing.

I don't know, you may be saying that this thing [your vision] that you want to accomplish is only for the White people or the Black people, No, No. Please don't be intimidated by the vision or dream that seems bigger than you, it is from God.

That is why the Bible says in Matt 11 vs. 28-30 *'...Come unto me all ye that labor and are heavy laden, and I will give you rest. Take my yoke upon you and learn of me for I am meek and lowly in heart: and ye shall find rest unto your souls, for my yoke is easy and my burden is light...'*

Our Lord Jesus Christ passed through a background with a very bad reputation and he overcame it, which is why I believe that every one with a background of bad reputation, whether you are Black or White, you will overcome it in Jesus name.

I prophesy by the Spirit of the living God that before Jesus comes, you will bless your world and I will bless my world in Jesus name, [Amen] Giving your life to Jesus Christ is the only key that opens the door to blessing your world.

By giving your life to Him, blessing your world is sure and guaranteed. Please say after me, Lord Jesus, I accept you today as my Lord and Savior, please come into my life and be my Lord in Jesus mighty name I pray [Amen] Shalom. Congratulations, you are now in Christ.

In blessing your world there is a need to talk about solution. Many people today, the plan of God for them is to bless their world and to do something glorious in their lifetime, but due to issues of life or challenges facing them, they are very far from the will and purpose of God for their lives.

Also maybe you might have experienced a background with a bad reputation, don' t worry; there is a solution for you!

First of all, what is a solution? The word solution has different definitions and meanings. Solution can be defined as a:

- substance that can be introduced in the midst of a circumstance
- vital object being used at the verge of a breakthrough

- method applied to solve a particular or major problem

Solution can also be defined as a way out of a tight corner.

I will share two stories with you about those who got solutions to their problems. The first story is about a widow in the Book of 2 Kings.

Now in 2 Kings 4 vs. 1-7, there is a story,

"...now there cried a certain woman of the wives of the sons of the prophet unto Elisha, saying, Thy servant my husband is dead; and thou knowest that that thy servant did fear the LORD: and the creditor is come to take unto him my two sons to be bondmen, vs2,

And Elisha said unto her, What shall I do for thee? Tell me, what hast thou in the house? And she said, Thine handmaid hath not any things in the house save a pot of oil vs3, Then he said, Go, borrow thee vessels abroad of all thy neighbors, even empty vessels, borrow not a few, vs4, And when thou art come in, thou shalt shut the door upon thee and upon thy sons, and shalt pour out into all those vessels, and thou shalt set aside that which is full. Vs5, so she went from him, and shut the door on her and upon her son, who brought the vessels to her: and she poured out. Vs6, and it came to pass, when the vessels were full that she said unto her son, bring me yet a vessel.

And he said unto her, there is not a vessel more, and the oil stayed. vs7, Then she came and told the men of God, and he said, Go, sell the oil, and pay thy debts, and live thou and thy Children of the rest.

Where we just read now, we can see that the wife of the prophet was passing through a famine. It was a very difficult time of her life, and in vs1, my Bible says she cried out to the man of God for her deliverance.

She said, thy servant my husband is dead: and the creditor is come to take unto him my two sons to be bondmen. She had no one to bail her out from her difficulties, she discovered that the only way out is by crying out to God for her solution.

And in vs2, the man of God asked her, what shall I do for thee? Beloved the way out from a famine or a problem that looks so difficult or horrible is by crying out to God.

Well you may be looking for help for coming out of that major problem or difficulty and it seems that there is no way out of it, just like the wife of the prophet she might have been looking for solution to her problem, going from one place to another to solve her problem.

But with all her efforts it seemed that there was no result at all, even her family had no answer to her problem. She might even have been trying to get a loan from the government or from the bank to enable her to solve her problem of debts, but all efforts did not work out.

They had no answer to her difficulties, but just like today at this hour, my Bible says in vs1, NOW. In my own words, NOW means, having tried every means possible without a tangible result, but yielding to a profane way of getting things done. Also NOW can mean I' m ready.

According to the dictionary point of view, NOW is defined as:

- the matter at hand
- momentary present
- It is a good time to do something
- It worked up to right now.

Vs1 says ...now, there cried a certain woman... Beloved, without a problem or famine there will not be a need for solution. I don´t know what that problem or difficulty is that you have been going through; I beseech you to cry out to God for your solution.

Fine, you may not know how the problem came to be, the famine may not be with your own consent but you find yourself in it, just like the wife of the prophet. She is not the one particularly in debts but her husband left debts for her when he died since he did not know that he was going to die.

Even looking at it as a Black man or someone from an African setting, the problem facing some group of people have to do with their foundation, culture, tradition or from the family they came out from, but as a person you find yourself in the midst of difficulties and it looks like solution is far from you.

I beseech you to hand over that battle to God and cry out for help, just like the woman did, The Lord God is asking someone today, what do you want? Just like the man of God ask the widow.

Are you tired of solving that problem alone? The Bible says in Psalms 55 vs22, *"...Cast thy burden upon the Lord, and He shall sustain thee: He shall never suffer the righteous to be moved..."* Also In 1 peter 5 Vs7, *"...Casting all your cares upon him: for He careth for you..."* The Lord God wants to give you rest from all your difficulties if only you can allow him.

And Elisha the man of God asked, what has thou in the house? And she replied nothing save a pot of oil.

Hmm, there is something magnificent in you, something glorious that the whole world is waiting for. But unknown to you, you think it is a child play or it is so little that you wonder if any good thing can come out of it. Well the man of God said to her, what is in thy house, Beloved there is something in you, please don´t kill it. It is your tool for the destiny that God has given to you to bless your world.

No matter how little it may look, believe in it and in your dream. That is your future. And in vs3, the hour of her solution came, the man of God said to her, Go, borrow thee vessels abroad of all thy neighbor´s, even empty vessels, borrow not a few, vs4, And when thou art come in, thou shalt shut the door upon thee and upon thy son, and shalt pour out into all those vessels, and thou shalt set aside that which is full. Beloved your God is a God of multiplication.

A jar of oil was multiplied to something great and she became one of the major suppliers of oil in her days. She followed all the instruction given to her.

Following instructions given to you by a man of God in time of famine or in time of need makes a lot of difference. I pray that the hour of solution you have been waiting for has come. And you will not know shame in the mighty name of Jesus.

WHAT CAN I DO IN TIME OF FAMINE THAT WILL BRING SOLUTION INTO MY LIFE

1. Learn how to cry out 2king 4 vs. 1
2. Learn how to lean on Jesus 2 king 4 vs. 1
3. Follow the instructions given to you 2 king 4 vs. 3
4. Be a peace maker, that is don´t shut all doors 2 king 4 vs. 3
5. Be creative 2 king 4 vs. 6

HOW TO MAINTAIN MY VICTORY AFTER SOLVING A MAJOR FAMINE OR PROBLEM

1. Be thankful of last victory Psalms50 vs. 14, Phil 4 vs. 6
2. Invest in the future and in people
3. Be a giver Psalms 24 vs. 9, Ecc 11 vs. 1,2
4. Pay your tithe Mal 3 vs. 10
5. Be creative.

The second story can be found in the book of Genesis, chapter 32 vs. 24-30. It says "...and Jacob was left alone; and there wrestled a man with him until the breaking of the day, vs25, and when he saw that he prevailed not against him, he touched the hallow of his thigh, and the hallow of Jacob's thigh was out of joint, as he *wrestled with him vs,26, And he said, let me go for the day breath, And he said, I will not let thee go, except thou bless me, vs27, And he said unto him, what is thy name? And he said, Jacob, vs, 28, And he said, Thy name shall be no more Jacob, but Israel. For as a prince hast thou power with God and with men, and hast prevailed, vs29, And Jacob asked him, and said, Tell me, I pray thee, thy name, And he said, wherefore is it that thou dost ask my name? And he blessed him there. Vs, 30, And Jacob called the name of the place penile: for I have seen God face to face, and my life is preserved..."* Verse 24 says Jacob was left alone.

WHY? What went wrong? Why was he left alone and what happened that made Jacob to be left alone? Something might have gone wrong.

In Genesis 25 vs. 20, shed more light to what make Jacob to be left alone.

Jacob defrauded his brother Esau, and corning take away his birthright from him, And the Bible says in, Chapter 32 Vs 24, that Jacob was left alone.

Are you like Jacob? People have forgotten you, saying that they will leave you to die with that problem or you may have been forgotten by your family, friend and relations saying no help for you at all, maybe your past sin is after you just like Jacob, there is a way out for you today if only you can go to God.

I promise you the problem will be over and you will bless your world. And the angel of the Lord blessed him and the story turn around, maybe you thought that all hope has gone and you about to pick it up and give up on your vision and in your sweet dream that God has giving you.

And you are saying after all can God forgive me? Beloved God can forgive, It those not matter the stated you are now, as a person. And what you have done in the pass, fine what you have done may look so terrible and horrible, and you are thinking can you ever get help at all.

Or can God forgive, God is a loving father and he forgives the sin of his Children. He visits Jacob despite what he has done in the past, and he turn is story around for good.

The plain and purpose of God for any man born of women is to make an impact in their word, God is not happy if any man dies without achieving his or her purpose in Life.

We are all born for a reasons and purpose; the only things that can hinder the plain of God for someone Life is sin. As we can see in the cased of Jacob, sin brings demarcation between God and men.

But there came a particular time in Jacob Life that he discovered the only way out from his problem that can brings solution into his Life, is by surrender everything to the hand of the most high God, He is a man that was rejected by Friends, family member and no one want to be known with him, because of his dubious ways.

Beloved are you like Jacob that people have written off? And they don't want to be known with you, just because of what you have done in the past, and you have left alone for years.

Also you are even thinking the end has come, but I'm here to let you know that the Almighty God have not writing you off yet, He love you more than you ever imagine is your loving Father he want the best for you and he care about you.

If only you can humble yourself and find his face and pray that he should have mercy on you, he will answer you, I know this not your end, they are still more things to be done by you. And I see you moving forward and making wonderful Impact in your world God bless you.

ACTION POINT

The only key that can open the door to blessing your world whether you are Black or White is by giving your Life to our Lord Jesus Christ. By giving your life to Him, blessing your world is sure and

guaranteed. Please say after me, Lord Jesus Christ I come to you today to drop all my wicked ways before you and I accept you as my personal Lord and Savior, I say no to sin again. I'm now washed in the pool of the blood of Jesus Christ. I confess I'm now a new man in Christ in Jesus name. [Amen]

Congratulations: You are now a new man in Christ Jesus.

The children

Of Zebedee.

''Knowledge involved in fact, and fact and knowledge! Work in hand toward a meaning, which defines a meaningful meaning. To imitate, as an imitator's? Is about fact! That is truth. Which at the process ending? There will always be a result or achievement''

(Mark 10:35 NKJV). Then James and John the son of Zebedee, come to Him, saying, Teacher, we want you to do for us whatever we ask.

''The children of Zebedee's.

''Beckon into the imitating endeavor's displayed by the children of Zebedee's from the beginning, immediate and to the ending of the imitating process? Giving the fact that the children of Zebedee are brothers that have been able to know more of some things being brothers, and knowing what that is a good quality of things, which been discovered by them.

Signified their brotherly relationship and time that they had spent together.

Without not be close or being a brothers? There will be some form of doubt, when beckon to imitate splendors process in the imitating process. Because of the reputation that is involved? Every one that seeks to imitate in life always being careful to know who and what is involved in what they want to imitate.

''*Carefully to know, who to imitate.*

No one that start the journey to imitate in life, that does not first got some important information in what that are involved in the surrounding that they want to explore.

Everyone had some information or what they see as some qualities before began their imitating process.

Also, Imitators are sight full, careful and obedient and they are not a novices that does not had some qualities information in the process that they wish to involved with.

Likewise, the children of Zebedee's that one of their brethren beckons them to the process are sight full, careful and obedient. Which has the immediate principles of involving in the substantial process of imitating a reputable role model.

''*Reputable role model.*

There are role model and there are role model in the imitating process. That when first sighting into their diligences or what is involved in what they want or thought to become an upcoming imitators? When first sighting to all what are involved in their process and their reputation! One will find out that, is just a wasting

of time and fraudulent
personality in the process
of imitating a role model.

Lord Jesus Christ, as a
role model? Sighting unto
him by the children of
Zebedee's, they were able
to discovered and finding
the substantial reputation
in a role model in the
imitating process.

Prayer: the grace to see
carefully in your first
sighting into a role model,
in any imitating process

that you will be involved
with, in Jesus name. Amen.

''Beckon into the imitating
endeavor's displayed by the
children of Zebedee's from
the beginning, immediate and
to the ending of the
imitating process? Giving
the fact that, the children
of Zebedee's are brothers
that have been able to know
more of some things being
brothers.

''The children of Zebedee's
are in one accord.

''In one accord is one of the elements or sources that enables an imitator's and a role model that an imitators imitate in the imitating process, to have a good process from the imitating immediate process to the achieving ending.

As other elements are substantially important in the imitating process! Likewise, to be in one accord also essentially important for any imitators that is in imitating process to achieve a good ending from the immediate process to the finishing ending.

Finishing ending! Is the glorious awaiting that every imitators always had in their mind, no one that is in the imitating environments and that wishes not to attain to the glorious ending in their discipline, Every one that imitate always has these in their mind, foresight and

in their diligently that
they are into.

Meanwhile, as every
endeavor, disciplines that
anyone or humans engaged
with in their environment?
Either in career, business
or other engagements? There
is always some elements and
an important object that
are essentially important
in order to achieve a
glorious ending.

''**The children of Zebedee's
are having the rightful
elements before imitating.**

As every imitators that I have been able to mentioned, from the beginning of the series till now! They displayed these substantial elements down from Elisha, Joshua and the disciples of Jesus.

Before attaining to the glorious ending in their endeavors. Nor of those that was able to mention or discovered in the scripture or in our surrounding that does not having or utilize these elements or object that are involved in the imitating process to the finishing ending.

''*Elements, object in the imitating process.*

We cannot do away with all these mechanisms that are involved in a process either to imitate, involving in other discipline that surround career or learning how some things are form, made or shaped.

Not involving or engaged with the elements will leads the immediate and ending to be futile.

Prayer: the grace to be involved substantial in every engagements you are into either in imitating, business, career or any glorious things you are into. In Jesus name. Amen.

''In one accord is one of the elements or sources that enables an imitators and a role model that an imitators imitate in the *imitating immediate process to the achieving ending.*

The children of Zebedee's are the examples of an upcoming imitators.

''Has I have mentioned in the previous series, that the secret of success at time! Is not what we are able to learn or acquired that enables us to be an achievers.

But the courage and zeal to move and taking a risks. Also, the risks that we took? Enables us to be achievers at times.

By the courage and risks displayed by the children of Zebedee's, gives some example of upcoming imitators in the imitating disciples.

Every upcoming imitator? All has some kind of uniqueness, which is different from any activities, and how humans are involved in doing some activities which involve disciplines in humans world? And the ways of their approaches is all different from every imitator that has even been in the imitating activities.

Therefore, some examples is Elisha, the way of his approaching is different from other's which I have been able to mentioned in our normal world and setting.

No one that has ever be in the imitating disciplines that follow normal trance of imitating? They all has different ways of their approaches and how they are in the imitating endeavours.

''Normal ways of approaching in the imitating disciples.

Thoughtful, there should be a normal way of approaching in the imitating endeavours! Such as the way things has been running in our normal ways of life. In terms of human's daily activities.

But in the imitating surroundings? Is much more different in our humans daily activities, has been running. In imitating? It has to do with divinely, and different ways of sighting into a role model by upcoming imitators

''Different ways of sighting by an imitator's into the imitating process.

Some imitator's, their sighting into a role model is different to other upcoming imitators.

To some, it maybe the leadership skills that they saw in a role model, that admire their attention into the imitating process.

Some, it may be the anointing of the role model which endowed by God in the life of the role model which admire the upcoming imitator's attention into the imitating process, while to some the characters of such role model admire their attention into the imitating process.

Prayer: may you have a right sighting in choosing a right role model in Jesus name. Amen

''Every upcoming, imitators? All has some

kind of uniqueness, which is different from any activities.

The children of Zebedee's approaching a role model.

''After sighting into a role model which meant one admired needs in a reputable role model? There will be a one to one relationship which will not give way to any hidden feeling or thoughts that does not has a good healthy in any relationship between a role model or an imitator's.

The children of Zebedee's have choosing a right reputable role model in their sighting in the imitating immediate and future discipline.

Which enables them to approach their role model in

what they want, admire and
want to obtain in their
disciplines.

To imitate as an imitator's
in the imitating process!
From the first sighting into
a role model? There must be
some kind of uniqueness
qualities that such imitators
has been wanted to achieved
or obtained. There is no
imitator's that want to
imitate in any imitating
disciplines that doesn't has
with in them, what they want
to obtain, want or admire to
achieve from their first
sighting into the imitating
discipline.

''The children of Zebedee's, what they admire to achieve.

As have mentioned that every
imitators that is in the
imitating disciplines, all
has their ways of approaching

in the imitating process, and their sighting into a role model always different from any other imitators, that has ever be in the imitating disciplines.

Likewise, their needs, wants and what they admire to achieve is different from any other's imitators in the imitating process.

To some Disciples of Christ that were with Christ, imitate him! All has their wants and what they admire to achieved in imitating Christ,

''Without a need, want and admire to achieve.

There is always need to imitate, imitating process is not a blank process that does not involved in a needs, want or what to admire to achieved.

As every diligences of men in humans world, has a needs which the diligences as been involved with materialization of result. Likewise, the imitating process involved in a need, want and what to admire in achieving.

In other words, every imitator are unique personality which wishes to imitate in the imitating process.

Prayer: your right needs, wants and admire to achieve in your imitating process will be achieved by you, in Jesus name. Amen.

''After sighting into a role model, which meant one admirable needs in a reputable role model, there

will be a one to one relationship.

The children of Zebedee's approaching a role model.

''Without a healthy relationship in any process, either in imitating or involving in any process? There will not be any gracious result. As every process that involved in having a result, needs a healthy relationship to materialize in a gracious result.

Likewise, the imitating process needs a healthy relationship for a gracious result.

A healthy relationship between the director of an organization and the subordinate in their duties of profession? Yielding to substantial result in their immediate and in their ending of their process.

Meanwhile, as a healthy relationship between the director of an organization and the followers is much needed in achieving result.

Also, a healthy relationship between a head of department in any government institution between their subordinate is also much needed for a gracious result. Imitating can also be grouped for a profession as other institution that I have mentioned.

''*Profession and imitating.*

In the early series, I have mentioned an imitator's as some one that has a good sighting, careful and some one that, that has a foresight into the immediate of the process that they are imitating.

Also, they are not novices that don't has an understanding in the surrounding of their disciplines. In other words, imitating process? Is also a Profession! Like other profession that can be discovered in human world and surroundings.

The Disciples of Christ, they didn't engage in any process, they imitate Christ and they follow him. Profession and imitating can be grouped as one area of disciples.

Every relevant being that can be discovered in human's surroundings and environment? They all have a profession.

Profession is a career that one has been able to be trained or has a knowledge in such career in order not to be irrelevant in human's environment and surrounding.

''Relevant and not to be irrelevant.

An imitator that imitates a role model, they are not irrelevant but relevant in humans surrounding and environments. They carried along the continuity they have been able to learn in their process or what they has been divinely impacted with in their process.

Continuity is one of the pillars in imitating between an imitators and a role model.

Prayer: divine success in your profession, in Jesus name.

''**Without a healthy relationship in any process, either to imitate or involving in any** *process! There will not be any gracious result.*

The children of Zebedee's are in a healthy profession.

''To be relevant, can be trace in doing something and being a doer, someone that does something. A doer is relevant and they are either imitating or involving in a profession.

Has I have mentioned that, imitating and profession can be grouped as one area of discipline, likewise to be irrelevant, not being a doer or involving in any disciplines? Makes, such life a circle of mountainous event and idle personnel.

The Bible do mentioned the diligent! That they will sit before kings and princes.

The children of Zebedee's, they are diligent and relevant and a doer; which makes them to have healthy conversation with Christ, and being diligent, relevant and a doer makes them successful imitators in the imitating process.

Meanwhile, if they are irrelevant, not diligent and not a doer? They wouldn't have being in a healthy conversation with Christ.

Being relevant, diligent and being a doer are what that make healthy relationship in any process in humans disciplines.

''**Human discipline.**

Without human being in any discipline or to engage in any substantial area of duties? Life will not have a substantial meaning to any one that is not engaging in any process and things that has been invented wouldn't have be invented, if those that invent are not in any process or irrelevant and not doing something.

Be a doer! Life is about a process, being diligent and to be a doer, not one that

is folding his or her arms,
will ever be an achievers
imitators.

Meanwhile, at any fantastic
invention that can be
discovered in human's
societies, are the
disciplines of some group
of diligent that choose to
either imitate or engaged
in a certain process which
make them to be in the
group of profession, which
invent some magnificent
edifices in human word and
is surrounding.

''Human world and its surrounding.

Every diligent personnel can be discovered in humans surrounding? They have good qualities and value. Their diligences are what everyone can be benefit with at any time of needs.

Therefore, there are no qualities, value and eloquent object or substances! That as ever be discovered in human's societies that does not be made or invented by those that choose to either imitate or engaging in a process of profession. Life is about value and qualities.

Prayer: your area of value and qualities will be discovered by you in Jesus name. Amen.

''To be relevant can be trace in doing something and being a doer, someone that does something.

The children of Zebedee's utilize the imitating process.

''**Imitators can also be grouped as an inventor.** Some one that create a thing or utilize his or her creativities to invent some magnificent things that has not be discovered or seen in human's world.

An inventor, is not only some one that invent some object or things that has being used in humans surrounding! But an inventor can also be some one that utilize his or her process for a magnificent value or qualities that benefited them or humans societies.

The children of Zebedee utilize their process of imitating to ask Christ, what other disciples have not ever had in mind to ask Christ.

Their senses of creativity in utilizing their process differential them, from other imitators that are in the imitating process.

Also, not every imitators or those that are in a profession, has the abilities to invent or utilize their creativity to invent a quality value either for themselves or for humanity.

An inventors are not common, like others in a process! Although, they are in a process like others. At time, some that invent or utilize their process for some qualities value are being gifted by God or gotten inspiration from divine sources.

''Gifted by God, gotten an inspiration from a divine sources.

I wonder how our world would have being today, if everyone is an inventor or someone that utilize his or her creativity in their process either for themselves or for the benefit of humanity.

How eloquent, are some object that has been

invented that every humans in humans setting are having contact with or been used for their needs.

But when carefully identify the sources, which it has come from? One will discovered that are the creativity of some people either in a process or in a profession

''Creativity of some people in a profession.

Life is about creativity and these are what that

makes life a meaningful meaning to everyone. Without not being creative? Human's lives will be a dormant phenomenon.

And by creativities the humans lives was form and the foundation was laid. Creativity is substantial needed in imitating and in any profession.

Prayer: the grace to be creative will be endowed to you in Jesus name.

''Imitators can also be grouped as an inventor's. Someone that create a thing or utilize his or her creativity to invent some meaningful things that has not be discovered or seen in human's world.

The children of Zebedee's being gifted by God.

''Not every one that is imitating and not everyone can be known as an inventor.

The imitating process? Is a quality process that involves God and the quality of beings. Every one living under the surface of the heaven, has his or her qualities that has being endowed by God to achieved in life.

As some, are natural gifted by God, also some learn some skills in an academic institution in order to gain a quality value of life.

Some people has their area that their quality value has been making tremendous impact to humanity and making them an achievers in the atmosphere of great achievers.

Those that has the fundamental understanding of having the quality value of being skilled or gifted by God, has been known as an achievers.

An achievers are those that utilize the fundamentals principles which they have gotten in a discipline to make a success in life. Success is an edifice of life that distinguished between those that are an achievers and those that does achieved in life.

''*Success is an edifice of life.*

Without being successful in life? There will always be a question in the heart of one! What are his or her existences in life? What is he or her created for. Without not having an understanding of one's existence in life? Such question will always be a mysteries to solve.

The children of Zebedee's, has already being gifted by God to discover their existences, which is not an exigent circumstances for them to solve.

They find themselves in their destiny and they utilize every substantial purpose in their imitating process.

There is always a purpose of a man existences in

life! Not being able to discover it, will always be an urge circumstances to solve.

''*An exigent circumstances to solve.*

A circumstance has been known as a phenomenon or challenges that humans do go through in life. Also, not being able to discovered one area of purpose can be link to exigent circumstances to solve in one life.

But, when one has been able to draw water from the well of knowledge! As the psalmist did during his horrible circumstances, that to know one purpose or achieved one victory in one purpose in life! As to be knowledge, that all power belong to God and his the one that endowed one in achieving, not what one been able to learn from an institution in order to be an achievers in life.

Prayer: may you have an encounter with God Almighty in Jesus name.

''Not every one that is imitating, and not

everyone can be known as an inventors.

The children of Zebedee's find themselves in their destiny.

''Without one not being able to discover his or her purpose in life and the reasons of one existences! There will always be a circle of an event that does not yield to productivities of one destiny in one diligence.

Diligences involved in destiny achieving and achieving involved in destiny materialization. Therefore, not every diligence that materializes in destiny achieving.

One may be diligent! But it may not be the real things that God, has determine for one to achieved in life. Also, diligences that has be tune to the heavenly mandate of destiny achieving, is what that materialize in achieving

The children of Zebedee's find themselves in their destiny. They didn't dwell too long to discovered their destiny! Divinely they find themselves in their destiny.

Many may be diligent, in every seasons of the year, but it may not be there diligent that involved in their destiny materialization. The Bible do mentioned,

Do you see a man who excels in his work? He will stand before kings; He will not stand before unknown men. **Proverbs 22: 29**

''*Standing before kings.*

Are the diligences of purpose that materialize in destiny achieving. The children of Zebedee's could not have stood before Christ! If, they have not achieved their existences in destiny achieving.

Every destiny achievers, they are diligent and having a purpose and the reasons of their diligences and purpose of achieving their destiny.

Without a destiny? There is no reasons of a purpose and the diligences of achieving destiny.

Prayer: the grace to discover your purpose and the diligent in destiny achieving in Jesus name.

Amen. "Why Black why Not

White......

BOOKS WRITTEN BY SHALOM:

Getting a Big Break

Why Black why Not White

Lord you are my deliverer

More of you lord

Living beyond the limit

Secret of an Imitator

Vision and you

You will know

Reasons

Great Success

The secret of an Achiever

Dominion: Sermon

The key of Success: Sermon

Hour of Solution with Jesus: Sermon

BOOKS WRITTEN BY SHALOM:

Filter and taking away the chaff

Excellent God

The peculiar

The children of Zebedee

Free from the trapped

He call

Shalom is the director of;
Adebisi shalom leadership
institute, is a ministries which is
based in Rooihuiskraal
Centurion. And the C.E.O of
Adebisi Shalom Trading
Enterprises

South Africa.

For prayers and counselling?

Send your request to:
aslileadership@gmail.com

Website site: aste-sa.business.site